Teen's Hygiene 101

A Comprehensive Guide to Staying Fresh and Clean

Philip S. Williams

Copyright © 2024 by Philip S. Williams

All Rights Reserved.

No part of this book may be used or reproduced by any means, graphic, electronic, or mechanical, including photocopying, recording, taping, or by any information storage retrieval system without the written permission of the publisher.

TABLE OF CONTENT

Introduction to Hygiene..4
Daily Hygiene Routine...11
   Morning Routine...11
   Nighttime Routine... 14
   Tips for Staying Fresh All Day................................ 17
Skin Care Basics.. 22
   Identifying Your Skin Type...................................... 22
   Proper Cleansing, Moisturizing, and Sun Protection.. 25
Hair Care Tips... 33
   Washing and Conditioning Your Hair...................... 33
   Managing Common Hair Concerns........................ 41
   Styling Tips for Different Hair Types....................... 43
Oral Hygiene Essentials..**45**
   Brushing and Flossing Techniques........................ 45
   Proper Flossing Technique..................................... 48
   Importance of Regular Dental Checkups................ 51
   Frequency of Dental Checkups.............................. 53
   Benefits of Regular Dental Checkups..................... 55
Body Odour and Sweat Management...................... **58**
   Understanding Body Odour and Sweat................. 58

Choosing the Right Deodorant................................ 60
Tips for Staying Odour-Free..................................... 62
Additional Tips for Managing Sweat and Odour..... 66
Nail Care... 69
Importance of Nail Hygiene..................................... 69
Steps for Keeping Nails Trimmed............................ 71
Moisturizing and Protecting Nails............................ 73
Avoiding Nail Biting and Infections.......................... 74
Strategies to Stop Nail Biting................................... 75
Preventing Nail Infections.. 77
Maintaining Overall Nail Health............................... 79
Personal Hygiene During Puberty........................... 81
Understanding Bodily Changes............................... 81
Physical Changes in Puberty...................................81
Special Hygiene Tips for Boys and Girls................. 84
General Hygiene Tips for Both Boys and Girls....... 89
Clothing and Laundry Hygiene................................ 91
Choosing Clean Clothes.. 91
How to Properly Wash and Store Your Clothes...... 95
Storing Clothes.. 98
Hygiene on the Go.. 101
Hygiene Tips for School, Sports, and Travel........ 101
Building a Portable Hygiene Kit............................. 107

3

Introduction to Hygiene

Personal Hygiene Defined
Personal hygiene refers to the practices that individuals perform to maintain cleanliness and promote health. These practices include regular bathing, washing hands, brushing teeth, and wearing clean clothes. Maintaining personal hygiene helps prevent the spread of diseases and keeps individuals feeling fresh and confident.

Historical Context
Throughout history, societies have recognized the importance of hygiene. Ancient civilizations like the Greeks and Romans built elaborate bathhouses and practised regular bathing. Modern hygiene practices have evolved with advancements in medical knowledge, emphasising the prevention of disease and the promotion of overall well-being.

Health Benefits

- Disease Prevention: Good personal hygiene helps prevent the spread of germs and infections. Regular handwashing, for example, reduces the transmission of illnesses such as the flu, colds, and gastrointestinal infections.
- Skin Health: Proper hygiene practices, like regular bathing and skincare, help maintain healthy skin, preventing issues like acne, rashes, and fungal infections.
- Oral Health: Brushing and flossing teeth prevent cavities, gum disease, and bad breath, contributing to overall oral health.
- Reduced Body Odour: Regular bathing and the use of deodorants help control body odour, making social interactions more pleasant.

Psychological Benefits

- Enhanced Self-Esteem: Feeling clean and well-groomed boosts self-confidence and self-esteem. This is particularly important for teens, who are often navigating social dynamics and developing their self-identity.
- Social Acceptance: Good personal hygiene is essential for social interactions. Poor hygiene can lead to social isolation and embarrassment, affecting relationships with peers and family.
- Mental Well-being: Maintaining hygiene routines can contribute to mental well-being by providing a sense of control and routine. It can also be a form of self-care that promotes relaxation and stress relief.

How Hygiene Affects Your Health and Confidence

Physical Health

- Immune System Support: Consistent hygiene practices support the immune system by reducing the body's exposure to harmful pathogens. This helps the body stay strong and fight off infections more effectively.
- Chronic Condition Management: For individuals with chronic conditions like diabetes or eczema, good hygiene is crucial. It helps manage symptoms and prevent complications, ensuring better overall health.
- Infection Control: Regular hygiene practices, such as handwashing, significantly reduce the risk of infections, contributing to overall public health and personal safety.

Emotional and Psychological Health

- Self-Image: Good personal hygiene plays a crucial role in developing a positive self-image. When teens feel clean and well-groomed, they are more likely to

have a positive outlook on themselves and their abilities.
- Confidence in Social Settings: Teens often face social pressure and scrutiny from their peers. Maintaining good hygiene can reduce anxiety about body odour, bad breath, or skin issues, making social interactions more enjoyable and less stressful.
- Academic and Extracurricular Performance: Confidence gained from good hygiene can positively impact other areas of life, including academic performance and participation in extracurricular activities. Teens who feel good about themselves are more likely to engage fully in their interests and pursue their goals.

Long-Term Benefits

- Healthy Habits Formation: Developing good hygiene habits during the teenage years sets the foundation for a lifetime of

healthy practices. These habits contribute to long-term health and well-being, reducing the risk of health problems in adulthood.
- Professional and Personal Success: Good hygiene is essential for professional success. It affects how others perceive us and can influence job prospects and career advancement. Additionally, maintaining good hygiene fosters strong personal relationships, as people are more likely to connect with individuals who exhibit cleanliness and self-care.

Daily Hygiene Routine

Morning Routine

Start with a Shower

- Why: Showering in the morning helps wake you up, remove sweat and bacteria accumulated overnight, and refresh your skin.
- How: Use warm water and a mild soap. Focus on areas prone to sweating and odour, such as underarms, groyne, and feet. Rinse thoroughly to avoid soap residue.

Facial Cleanse

- Why: Cleansing your face removes oil and dirt that can clog pores and cause acne.
- How: Use a gentle cleanser suitable for your skin type. Rinse with lukewarm water and pat dry with a clean towel.

Brush Your Teeth

- Why: Oral hygiene prevents bad breath, cavities, and gum disease.
- How: Brush for at least two minutes using fluoride toothpaste. Don't forget to brush your tongue and floss between your teeth to remove plaque and food particles.

Deodorant Application

- Why: Deodorant helps control body odour and sweating throughout the day.
- How: Apply deodorant or antiperspirant to clean, dry underarms. Allow it to dry before dressing.

Skincare Routine

- Why: A proper skincare routine protects your skin from environmental damage and keeps it healthy.
- How: After cleansing, apply a moisturiser suited for your skin type. If you'll be outdoors, use a sunscreen with at least SPF 30 to protect against UV rays.

Hair Care

- Why: Keeping your hair clean and well-groomed prevents scalp issues and improves your appearance.
- How: Depending on your hair type, you may need to wash your hair daily or every few days. Use a gentle shampoo and conditioner. Style your hair as desired, ensuring it's free from knots and excess oil.

Dress in Clean Clothes

- Why: Wearing clean clothes prevents odour and skin irritation.
- How: Choose clothes appropriate for the weather and your activities for the day. Ensure your clothes are clean, wrinkle-free, and comfortable.

Nighttime Routine

Remove Makeup (if applicable)

- Why: Removing makeup prevents clogged pores and skin irritation.
- How: Use a gentle makeup remover or cleanser designed for your skin type. Follow up with your usual facial cleanser.

Brush and Floss Your Teeth

- Why: Maintaining oral hygiene before bed prevents plaque buildup and tooth decay.
- How: Brush your teeth for two minutes and floss thoroughly. Consider using a

mouthwash to kill bacteria and freshen your breath.

Nighttime Skincare

- Why: Nighttime is when your skin repairs and rejuvenates itself.
- How: Cleanse your face to remove any remaining dirt and oil. Apply a nighttime moisturiser or treatment product suited to your skin concerns, such as acne treatments or anti-aging serums.

Shower or Bath (Optional)

- Why: Taking a shower or bath before bed can relax you and help you sleep better.
- How: Use warm water and your preferred soap. Focus on relaxing and unwinding from the day.

Hair Care

- Why: Preparing your hair for bed prevents tangles and scalp issues.
- How: Brush or comb your hair to remove tangles. If your hair is long, consider braiding it to prevent knots. If you wash your hair at night, ensure it's completely dry before going to bed.

Hydrate and Relax

- Why: Staying hydrated and relaxing helps your body and mind prepare for restful sleep.
- How: Drink a glass of water to stay hydrated. Engage in a relaxing activity like reading or listening to calming music to wind down.

Tips for Staying Fresh All Day

Stay Hydrated

- Why: Drinking plenty of water keeps your skin hydrated and helps your body flush out toxins.
- How: Aim to drink at least 8 glasses of water a day. Carry a reusable water bottle with you to stay hydrated on the go.

Carry Hygiene Essentials

- Why: Having hygiene products on hand allows you to freshen up throughout the day.
- How: Pack a small hygiene kit with items like hand sanitizer, facial wipes, deodorant, and breath mints or gum.

Regular Hand Washing

- Why: Washing your hands reduces the spread of germs and prevents illness.
- How: Wash your hands with soap and water for at least 20 seconds, especially before eating and after using the restroom.

If soap and water aren't available, use hand sanitizer with at least 60% alcohol.

Reapply Deodorant

- Why: Reapplying deodorant helps manage sweat and odour during the day.
- How: If you're prone to sweating, carry a travel-size deodorant and reapply as needed.

Change Clothes if Necessary

- Why: Changing into fresh clothes can help you feel more comfortable and reduce odour.
- How: If you get sweaty or dirty during the day, bring a change of clothes to school or work.

Keep Your Face Clean

- Why: Keeping your face clean prevents acne and oil buildup.

- How: Use blotting papers or facial wipes to remove excess oil and sweat from your face. Avoid touching your face with dirty hands.

Freshen Breath

- Why: Maintaining fresh breath is crucial for confidence and social interactions.
- How: Brush your teeth after meals when possible. Carry sugar-free gum or mints to freshen your breath throughout the day.

Stay Active

- Why: Regular physical activity boosts circulation and energy levels, contributing to overall freshness.
- How: Take short breaks to move around, stretch, or go for a walk. This helps keep your body energised and prevents sluggishness.

Healthy Diet

- Why: Eating a balanced diet supports overall health and helps your body function optimally.
- How: Include plenty of fruits, vegetables, lean proteins, and whole grains in your diet. Avoid excessive sugar and junk food, which can affect your skin and energy levels.

Mindful Stress Management

- Why: Managing stress helps maintain overall well-being and reduces negative impacts on your hygiene.
- How: Practise stress-relief techniques like deep breathing, meditation, or exercise. Ensure you get enough sleep to help your body recover and stay fresh.

Skin Care Basics

Identifying Your Skin Type

Understanding your skin type is the first step in creating an effective skincare routine. There are five primary skin types: normal, oily, dry, combination, and sensitive. Each skin type has unique characteristics and needs.

Normal Skin

- Characteristics: Balanced, not too oily or dry, few imperfections, no severe sensitivity, and a radiant complexion.
- Care Tips: Use gentle products that maintain skin's natural balance. Regular cleansing, moisturising, and sun protection are essential.

Oily Skin

- Characteristics: Enlarged pores, shiny appearance, prone to blackheads and acne.
- Care Tips: Use oil-free and non-comedogenic products. Cleanse twice a day with a gentle cleanser to remove excess oil. Avoid heavy creams and opt for light, gel-based moisturisers.

Dry Skin

- Characteristics: Tightness, flakiness, rough texture, visible lines, and dull complexion.
- Care Tips: Use rich, hydrating products. Cleanse with a mild, moisturising cleanser and apply a thick, emollient moisturiser. Avoid hot water, which can strip the skin of its natural oils.

Combination Skin

- Characteristics: Oily in the T-zone (forehead, nose, and chin) and dry or normal on the cheeks.
- Care Tips: Use products tailored to different areas of your face. For example, apply a light moisturiser on the T-zone and a richer one on the cheeks. Gentle, balanced cleansers work best.

Sensitive Skin

Characteristics: Easily irritated, redness, itching, and prone to allergic reactions.
Care Tips: Use hypoallergenic and fragrance-free products. Test new products on a small patch of skin before full application. Avoid harsh chemicals and exfoliants.

Proper Cleansing, Moisturizing, and Sun Protection

1. **Cleansing**

Choose the Right Cleanser

- Normal Skin: Use a gentle foaming or gel cleanser.
- Oily Skin: Opt for a cleanser with salicylic acid or benzoyl peroxide to control oil and prevent acne.
- Dry Skin: Select a creamy, hydrating cleanser with ingredients like glycerin or hyaluronic acid.
- Combination Skin: Use a balanced cleanser that addresses both oily and dry areas.
- Sensitive Skin: Use a fragrance-free, hypoallergenic cleanser with soothing ingredients like aloe vera.

How to Cleanse

- Step 1: Wet your face with lukewarm water.

- Step 2: Apply the cleanser and gently massage it into your skin in circular motions, avoiding the eye area.
- Step 3: Rinse thoroughly with lukewarm water and pat dry with a clean towel.

Cleansing Tips

- Cleanse twice a day, in the morning and before bed, to remove dirt, oil, and makeup.
- Avoid over-cleansing, as it can strip the skin of natural oils and cause irritation.

1. Moisturizing

Choose the Right Moisturiser

- Normal Skin: Use a lightweight, hydrating moisturiser.
- Oily Skin: Opt for an oil-free, non-comedogenic moisturiser.

- Dry Skin: Select a rich, emollient moisturiser with ingredients like shea butter or ceramides.
- Combination Skin: Use a gel-based moisturiser for oily areas and a richer cream for dry areas.
- Sensitive Skin: Choose a fragrance-free, hypoallergenic moisturiser with soothing ingredients like chamomile or oatmeal.

How to Moisturize

- Step 1: Apply moisturiser to clean, damp skin to lock in moisture.
- Step 2: Use gentle, upward strokes to apply the product, avoiding the eye area unless using an eye cream.
- Step 3: Allow the moisturiser to absorb fully before applying any other products.

Moisturizing Tips

- Moisturise twice a day, in the morning and at night.

- Adjust the type of moisturiser based on seasonal changes; use lighter formulations in the summer and richer ones in the winter.

3. Sun Protection

Importance of Sun Protection

- Protecting your skin from the sun's harmful UV rays prevents premature ageing, sunburn, and skin cancer.

Choosing the Right Sunscreen

- SPF: Use a broad-spectrum sunscreen with at least SPF 30.
- Formulation: Choose a sunscreen suitable for your skin type. For example, use oil-free formulas for oily skin and hydrating ones for dry skin.
- Ingredients: Look for ingredients like zinc oxide or titanium dioxide for sensitive

skin, as they are less likely to cause irritation.

How to Apply Sunscreen

- Step 1: Apply sunscreen generously to all exposed skin 15-30 minutes before going outside.
- Step 2: Reapply every two hours, or more often if swimming or sweating.
- Step 3: Don't forget often-missed areas like the ears, neck, and tops of feet.

Sun Protection Tips

- Wear protective clothing, hats, and sunglasses for added protection.
- Seek shade during peak sun hours, typically from 10 a.m. to 4 p.m.
- Use sunscreen year-round, even on cloudy days, as UV rays can penetrate clouds.

Additional Skincare Tips

1. **Exfoliation**

   - Why: Exfoliating removes dead skin cells, unclogs pores, and promotes cell turnover.
   - How: Use a gentle exfoliant suitable for your skin type 1-3 times a week. Avoid over-exfoliating, which can irritate the skin.

Hydration

   - Why: Drinking enough water keeps your skin hydrated from the inside out.
   - How: Aim to drink at least 8 glasses of water a day. Eat hydrating foods like fruits and vegetables.

Healthy Diet

   - Why: A balanced diet supports overall skin health.
   - How: Consume a variety of nutrient-rich foods, including fruits, vegetables, lean proteins, and whole grains. Limit sugar

and processed foods, which can contribute to skin issues.

Avoiding Harmful Habits

- Why: Certain habits can negatively impact your skin.
- How: Avoid smoking and excessive alcohol consumption, which can lead to premature ageing and skin damage. Get adequate sleep to allow your skin to repair and rejuvenate.

Hair Care Tips

Washing and Conditioning Your Hair

Proper washing and conditioning are essential for maintaining healthy hair and scalp. They remove dirt, oil, and product buildup, while providing moisture and nutrients to keep hair strong and manageable.

Washing Your Hair

1. Choosing the Right Shampoo

- Normal Hair: Use a mild, balanced shampoo that cleanses without stripping natural oils.
- Oily Hair: Opt for a clarifying shampoo that removes excess oil and buildup.

- Dry Hair: Choose a moisturising shampoo with hydrating ingredients like shea butter or glycerin.
- Curly Hair: Use a sulphate-free, hydrating shampoo that preserves natural oils and moisture.
- Colour-Treated Hair: Select a colour-safe shampoo that protects and maintains colour vibrancy.

How to Wash Your Hair

- Step 1: Wet your hair thoroughly with lukewarm water.
- Step 2: Apply a quarter-sized amount of shampoo to your scalp and massage gently with your fingertips, not your nails.
- Step 3: Work the shampoo through the lengths of your hair without piling it on top of your head, which can cause tangling.
- Step 4: Rinse thoroughly, ensuring no shampoo residue is left.

Washing Frequency

- Normal Hair: Wash every 2-3 days.
- Oily Hair: Wash everyday or every other day.
- Dry Hair: Wash 1-2 times a week.
- Curly Hair: Wash 1-2 times a week or as needed to maintain moisture balance.
- Colour-Treated Hair: Wash 2-3 times a week to preserve colour.

2. Conditioning Your Hair

Choosing the Right Conditioner

- Normal Hair: Use a lightweight conditioner that provides moisture without weighing hair down.
- Oily Hair: Choose a light, oil-free conditioner and apply only to the ends of your hair.
- Dry Hair: Opt for a rich, hydrating conditioner with ingredients like argan oil or coconut oil.

- Curly Hair: Use a deep-conditioning treatment that defines curls and reduces frizz.
- Colour-Treated Hair: Select a conditioner designed to protect and maintain colour-treated hair.

How to Condition Your Hair

- Step 1: Apply conditioner to the mid-lengths and ends of your hair, avoiding the scalp to prevent greasiness.
- Step 2: Use a wide-tooth comb or your fingers to distribute the conditioner evenly and detangle your hair.
- Step 3: Leave the conditioner in for 2-5 minutes to allow it to penetrate the hair shaft.
- Step 4: Rinse thoroughly with cool or lukewarm water to seal the hair cuticle and add shine.

Deep Conditioning and Treatments

- Frequency: Use a deep conditioning treatment or hair mask once a week for dry, damaged, or colour-treated hair.
- How to Use: Apply the treatment to clean, damp hair, focusing on the ends. Leave it on for the recommended time (usually 10-30 minutes) before rinsing thoroughly.

Managing Different Hair Types and Styles

Straight Hair

- Characteristics: Straight hair is often sleek and shiny but can be prone to oiliness and lack of volume.
- Care Tips:
- Use a volumizing shampoo and conditioner to add body.
- Avoid heavy styling products that can weigh down the hair.
- Use a heat protectant before using hot tools to prevent damage.

Wavy Hair

- Characteristics: Wavy hair has a natural wave pattern and can range from loose to more defined waves. It can be prone to frizz and uneven texture.
- Care Tips:
- Use a sulphate-free, hydrating shampoo and conditioner.
- Apply a lightweight mousse or curl-enhancing cream to define waves.
- Air-dry or use a diffuser to enhance natural waves without causing frizz.

Curly Hair

- Characteristics: Curly hair has defined curls and tends to be dry and frizzy. It requires more moisture and gentle handling.
- Care Tips:
- Use a moisturising shampoo and deep conditioner.

- Avoid brushing dry curls to prevent frizz and breakage. Use a wide-tooth comb or fingers to detangle when wet.
- Apply a leave-in conditioner and curl-defining gel or cream to enhance and define curls.
- Consider the "plopping" method for drying, which involves using a T-shirt or microfiber towel to scrunch and define curls without frizz.

Coily/Kinky Hair

- Characteristics: Coily or kinky hair has tight, small curls or coils and is prone to dryness and shrinkage. It requires intensive moisture and care.
- Care Tips:
- Use a sulphate-free, moisturising shampoo and deep conditioner.
- Regularly apply leave-in conditioners, oils, and butters to lock in moisture.

- Detangle gently with fingers or a wide-tooth comb when hair is wet and conditioned.
- Protective styles, such as braids or twists, can help reduce breakage and retain length.

Managing Common Hair Concerns

Frizz Control

- Use anti-frizz serums or creams to smooth the hair cuticle.
- Avoid over-washing and use a hydrating shampoo and conditioner.
- Sleep on a silk or satin pillowcase to reduce friction and frizz.

Heat Damage Prevention

- Limit the use of heat styling tools like blow dryers, flat irons, and curling irons.

- Always apply a heat protectant spray or serum before using hot tools.
- Opt for air-drying or low-heat settings whenever possible.

Split Ends and Breakage

- Get regular trims every 6-8 weeks to remove split ends.
- Use a wide-tooth comb to detangle hair gently, starting from the ends and working your way up.
- Avoid tight hairstyles that pull on the hair and cause breakage.

Hair Loss and Thinning

- Maintain a healthy diet rich in vitamins and minerals that support hair growth, such as biotin, vitamin E, and iron.
- Avoid harsh chemical treatments and excessive heat styling.

- Consult a dermatologist or trichologist if hair loss persists to rule out underlying conditions.

Styling Tips for Different Hair Types

Straight Hair

- Add volume with a round brush while blow-drying.
- Use a flat iron for a sleek, polished look or create waves by twisting sections of hair around the iron.

Wavy Hair

- Enhance natural waves with a sea salt spray or texturizing spray.
- Use a curling following wand to define waves and create a beachy, tousled look.

Curly Hair

- Define curls with a curl-enhancing cream or gel.
- Use a diffuser attachment on your blow dryer to dry curls gently and maintain their shape.

Coily/Kinky Hair

- Experiment with protective styles like braids, twists, and buns to protect hair from damage and promote growth.
- Use styling gels or creams to define coils and reduce frizz.

Oral Hygiene Essentials

Brushing and Flossing Techniques

Brushing Your Teeth

Choosing the Right Toothbrush

- Bristle Type: Use a toothbrush with soft bristles to avoid damaging your gums and enamel.
- Size: Choose a toothbrush with a small head to easily reach all areas of your mouth.
- Electric vs. Manual: Both can be effective if used correctly, but electric toothbrushes often remove more plaque and reduce gingivitis more effectively.

Selecting the Right Toothpaste

- Fluoride Toothpaste: Helps prevent cavities and strengthens enamel.
- Whitening Toothpaste: Can remove surface stains but should not be abrasive.
- Sensitive Toothpaste: Contains ingredients like potassium nitrate to reduce tooth sensitivity.

Proper Brushing Technique

- Step 1: Apply a pea-sized amount of toothpaste to your toothbrush.
- Step 2: Hold the toothbrush at a 45-degree angle to your gums.
- Step 3: Use gentle, circular motions to brush the outer and inner surfaces of your teeth.
- Step 4: Brush the chewing surfaces with short back-and-forth strokes.
- Step 5: Brush your tongue to remove bacteria and freshen your breath.

- Step 6: Spit out the toothpaste, but don't rinse your mouth immediately to allow the fluoride to work.

Brushing Frequency

- Brush at least twice a day, in the morning and before bed, for two minutes each time.
- If possible, brush after meals to remove food particles and reduce plaque buildup.

Flossing Your Teeth

Choosing the Right Floss

- Waxed vs. Unwaxed: Waxed floss slides more easily between tight teeth, while unwaxed floss may be thinner and better for larger gaps.
- Dental Tape: Thicker and flatter than regular floss, ideal for people with wider spaces between their teeth.

- Floss Picks: Convenient for on-the-go use but may not be as effective as regular floss in removing all plaque.

Proper Flossing Technique

- Step 1: Use about 18 inches of floss and wind most of it around each middle finger, leaving an inch or two to work with.
- Step 2: Hold the floss tightly between your thumbs and forefingers.
- Step 3: Gently slide the floss between your teeth using a gentle sawing motion.
- Step 4: Curve the floss around each tooth in a C shape and slide it under the gumline.
- Step 5: Move the floss up and down to remove plaque and food particles.
- Step 6: Use a clean section of floss for each tooth.

Flossing Frequency

- Floss at least once a day, preferably before bedtime, to remove plaque and food particles from between your teeth where your toothbrush can't reach.

Additional Oral Hygiene Practices

Mouthwash

- Antiseptic Mouthwash: Helps kill bacteria that cause plaque, gingivitis, and bad breath.
- Fluoride Mouthwash: Provides additional protection against cavities and strengthens enamel.
- How to Use: Swish the recommended amount in your mouth for 30-60 seconds after brushing and flossing.

Tongue Cleaning

- Why: Removing bacteria from the tongue helps prevent bad breath and improves overall oral hygiene.

- How: Use a tongue scraper or your toothbrush to gently clean your tongue from back to front.

Chewing Gum

- Sugar-Free Gum: Chewing sugar-free gum after meals stimulates saliva production, which helps neutralise acids and wash away food particles.
- Xylitol: Gum containing xylitol can help reduce the risk of cavities.

Hydration

- Why: Staying hydrated helps maintain saliva flow, which is essential for washing away food particles and bacteria.
- How: Drink plenty of water throughout the day, especially after eating.

Importance of Regular Dental Checkups

Why Regular Dental Checkups Matter

Early Detection of Problems

- Cavities: Dentists can identify and treat cavities early, preventing them from becoming more serious and painful.
- Gum Disease: Regular checkups allow for the early detection and treatment of gum disease, which can prevent tooth loss and other complications.
- Oral Cancer: Dentists perform oral cancer screenings to detect any signs of cancer early, improving the chances of successful treatment.

Professional Cleaning

- Plaque and Tartar Removal: Professional cleanings remove plaque and tartar

buildup that cannot be removed by regular brushing and flossing.
- Stain Removal: Cleanings help remove surface stains, resulting in a brighter smile.
- Gum Health: Regular cleanings help prevent gum disease and maintain healthy gums.

Preventive Care

- Sealants: Dentists can apply dental sealants to the chewing surfaces of back teeth to prevent cavities.
- Fluoride Treatments: Professional fluoride treatments strengthen enamel and prevent cavities.
- Education: Dentists provide personalised advice on proper brushing and flossing techniques, diet, and other oral hygiene practices.

Frequency of Dental Checkups

Routine Checkups

- Every Six Months: Most people should visit the dentist twice a year for a checkup and cleaning. This frequency helps maintain optimal oral health and catch any issues early.
- Personalised Schedule: Depending on your oral health, your dentist may recommend more frequent visits. For example, if you have a history of gum disease or are at high risk for cavities, you may need to visit every 3-4 months.

Signs You Need a Dental Checkup

- Tooth Pain: Persistent tooth pain can indicate a cavity, infection, or other dental issues that need professional attention.
- Bleeding Gums: Gums that bleed regularly, especially when brushing or flossing, can be a sign of gum disease.

- Persistent Bad Breath: Bad breath that doesn't improve with proper oral hygiene may indicate an underlying problem.
- Mouth Sores: Sores that don't heal within a week or two should be evaluated by a dentist.
- Changes in Bite: If your bite feels different or if you notice any changes in your teeth alignment, see your dentist.

Benefits of Regular Dental Checkups

Cost Savings

- Preventive Care: Regular checkups help prevent serious dental problems that can be more costly and time-consuming to treat.
- Early Treatment: Addressing dental issues early can save money on extensive

treatments, such as root canals or extractions.

Overall Health

- Oral-Systemic Link: Poor oral health is linked to various systemic health issues, including heart disease, diabetes, and respiratory infections. Maintaining good oral hygiene and regular dental visits contribute to overall health.
- Nutrition: Healthy teeth and gums are essential for proper chewing and digestion, which supports overall nutrition and well-being.

Confidence and Self-Esteem

- Healthy Smile: A healthy, bright smile boosts confidence and self-esteem.
- Fresh Breath: Regular dental care helps maintain fresh breath, which is important for social interactions and self-assurance.

Body Odour and Sweat Management

Understanding Body Odour and Sweat

What Causes Body Odour?

- Sweat: Produced by sweat glands, sweat itself is odourless. However, when sweat comes into contact with bacteria on the skin, it can produce an unpleasant smell.
- Bacteria: The main culprits of body odour are bacteria that break down sweat into acids. These bacteria thrive in warm, moist environments like the armpits and groyne.

- Apocrine Glands: Found in areas with hair follicles (armpits, scalp, and groyne), these glands produce sweat that contains proteins and lipids, which bacteria feed on, leading to odour.

Types of Sweat Glands

- Eccrine Glands: Found all over the body, these glands produce a watery sweat that helps regulate body temperature.
- Apocrine Glands: Located in specific areas (armpits, groyne, scalp), these glands produce a thicker sweat that can lead to odour when broken down by bacteria.

Choosing the Right Deodorant

Types of Deodorants and Antiperspirants

- Deodorants: Mask or neutralise body odour but do not prevent sweating. They

contain antimicrobial agents to reduce bacteria and fragrances to mask odour.
- Antiperspirants: Reduce sweating by temporarily blocking sweat glands. They contain aluminium-based compounds that form a gel-like barrier over sweat glands.
- Combination Products: Some products offer both deodorant and antiperspirant properties, providing odour control and reducing sweat.

Key Ingredients to Look For

- Antimicrobial Agents: Ingredients like triclosan and alcohol help reduce the bacteria that cause odour.
- Fragrances: Essential oils and synthetic fragrances mask unpleasant odours.
- Aluminium Compounds: Aluminium chloride and aluminium zirconium are common in antiperspirants to reduce sweating.
- Natural Ingredients: Baking soda, tea tree oil, and witch hazel are used in natural

deodorants to neutralise odour and reduce bacteria.

Choosing the Right Product for Your Needs

- Sensitivity: If you have sensitive skin, look for deodorants and antiperspirants labelled as hypoallergenic or formulated for sensitive skin, which typically exclude alcohol and strong fragrances.
- Activity Level: For those who sweat heavily or are very active, a strong antiperspirant with higher concentrations of aluminium compounds may be necessary.
- Natural Preferences: If you prefer natural products, look for deodorants without aluminium, parabens, and artificial fragrances. These often use baking soda, coconut oil, and essential oils.
- Long-Lasting Protection: For all-day protection, choose products labelled as "24-hour" or "long-lasting."

Tips for Staying Odour-Free

Daily Hygiene Practices

Shower Daily

- Why: Regular showers help remove sweat, bacteria, and dirt from your skin, reducing the potential for body odour.
- How: Use a gentle, antibacterial soap, focusing on areas prone to sweat, such as armpits, groyne, and feet.

Proper Drying

- Why: Bacteria thrive in moist environments, so thoroughly drying your skin after showering helps prevent bacterial growth.
- How: Use a clean, dry towel to pat your skin dry, paying extra attention to folds and creases where moisture can linger.

Clean Clothing

- Why: Wearing clean clothes helps prevent the buildup of sweat and bacteria that can cause odour.
- How: Change clothes daily, especially underwear and socks. Wash workout clothes after each use.

Shaving and Trimming

- Why: Hair can trap sweat and bacteria, leading to more odour. Shaving or trimming hair in areas like the armpits can help reduce this.
- How: Use a clean razor and shaving cream to avoid irritation. Trim hair with scissors or clippers if you prefer not to shave.

Diet and Hydration

Hydration

- Why: Staying hydrated helps regulate body temperature and reduce the concentration of odour-causing compounds in sweat.
- How: Drink plenty of water throughout the day, aiming for at least 8 glasses.

Dietary Choices

- Why: Certain foods can contribute to body odour, such as spicy foods, garlic, onions, and red meat.
- How: Reduce consumption of these foods if you notice they affect your body odour. Include plenty of fruits and vegetables, which can help improve body odour.

Additional Tips for Managing Sweat and Odour

Use Deodorant or Antiperspirant Correctly

- When: Apply deodorant or antiperspirant to clean, dry skin, ideally after showering.
- How: Ensure the product covers the entire area prone to sweating. Reapply as needed throughout the day.

Wear Breathable Fabrics

- Why: Natural fibres like cotton and moisture-wicking fabrics help keep your skin dry by allowing sweat to evaporate.
- How: Choose clothing made from these materials, especially during physical activity or hot weather.

Manage Stress

- Why: Stress can trigger increased sweating and body odour due to the activation of apocrine glands.
- How: Practise stress-reducing techniques such as deep breathing, meditation, or exercise to manage stress levels.

Foot Odour

- Why: Feet can produce significant odour due to sweat and bacteria buildup.
- How: Wash feet daily with antibacterial soap, dry thoroughly, and use foot powder or antiperspirant. Wear moisture-wicking socks and alternate shoes to allow them to dry out.

Freshen Up Throughout the Day

- Why: Freshening up can help manage sweat and odour during long or active days.
- How: Carry travel-size deodorant, wet wipes, or body spray to use as needed.

Nail Care

Importance of Nail Hygiene

- Prevents Infections: Keeping nails clean and trimmed prevents dirt and bacteria from accumulating under the nails, reducing the risk of infections.
- Promotes Health: Regular nail care promotes overall nail health and prevents common problems like ingrown nails and hangnails.
- Enhances Appearance: Well-maintained nails improve your overall appearance and can boost self-confidence.

Steps for Keeping Nails Clean

Regular Cleaning

- How: Wash your hands and feet regularly with soap and water, paying special attention to your nails. Use a soft nail brush to gently scrub under and around the nails.
- When: Clean your nails every day, especially after activities that can get them dirty, such as gardening, cooking, or playing sports.

Removing Debris

- How: Use a nail stick or a soft toothbrush to gently remove dirt and debris from under your nails. Be gentle to avoid damaging the nail or the skin underneath.
- When: Do this daily or as needed to keep your nails free from buildup.

Disinfecting Tools

- Why: Using clean tools helps prevent the spread of bacteria and infections.
- How: Regularly disinfect nail clippers, scissors, and other tools with rubbing alcohol or a disinfectant solution.

Steps for Keeping Nails Trimmed

Regular Trimming

- How: Use sharp, clean nail clippers or scissors to trim your nails straight across. For fingernails, leave them slightly rounded at the tips. For toenails, trim them straight across to prevent ingrown nails.
- When: Trim your nails every 1-2 weeks, or as needed to maintain a desired length and prevent them from becoming too long or breaking.

Filing Nails

- How: Use a nail file to smooth the edges of your nails after trimming. File in one direction to prevent splitting and weakening.
- When: File your nails after each trimming session or whenever you notice rough edges.

Cuticle Care

- How: Soak your nails in warm water to soften the cuticles. Gently push them back using a cuticle pusher. Avoid cutting the cuticles, as they protect the nail matrix from infections.
- When: Perform cuticle care once a week or as needed.

Moisturizing and Protecting Nails

Hydration

- Why: Keeping nails and cuticles moisturised prevents them from becoming dry and brittle.
- How: Apply hand cream, cuticle oil, or a moisturising lotion to your nails and cuticles regularly, especially after washing your hands.

Wearing Gloves

- Why: Protecting your nails from harsh chemicals and prolonged exposure to water can prevent damage and dryness.
- How: Wear gloves when doing household chores, such as washing dishes or cleaning, and when working with chemicals.

Avoiding Nail Biting and Infections

Causes of Nail Biting

- Stress and Anxiety: Many people bite their nails as a way to cope with stress and anxiety.
- Boredom: Nail biting can be a habit formed out of boredom or as a way to pass time.
- Perfectionism: Some individuals bite their nails to remove perceived imperfections or irregularities.

Consequences of Nail Biting

- Infections: Biting nails can introduce bacteria and viruses into your mouth, leading to infections.
- Damage to Nails: Chronic nail biting can damage the nail bed, leading to irregular nail growth and deformities.
- Dental Problems: Nail biting can cause teeth to chip, break, or become misaligned.

Strategies to Stop Nail Biting

Identify Triggers

- Why: Understanding what prompts you to bite your nails can help you develop strategies to avoid or manage those triggers.
- How: Keep a journal to track when and why you bite your nails, noting any patterns or specific triggers.

Keep Nails Short

- Why: Short nails are less tempting to bite and are more difficult to chew on.
- How: Regularly trim and file your nails to keep them short and smooth.

Use Bitter-Tasting Nail Polish

- Why: Applying a bitter-tasting nail polish can deter you from biting your nails due to the unpleasant taste.

- How: Apply the polish according to the product instructions and reapply as needed.

Find Alternatives

- Why: Replacing nail biting with a healthier habit can help break the cycle.
- How: Consider chewing gum, using a stress ball, or fidgeting with a small object to keep your hands and mouth occupied.

Practice Stress-Relief Techniques

- Why: Reducing stress can decrease the urge to bite your nails.
- How: Try relaxation techniques such as deep breathing, meditation, or yoga to manage stress and anxiety.

Preventing Nail Infections

Keep Nails Dry and Clean

- Why: Moist environments promote the growth of bacteria and fungi.
- How: Dry your hands and feet thoroughly after washing and avoid prolonged exposure to water.

Avoid Sharing Nail Tools

- Why: Sharing tools can spread bacteria and fungi, leading to infections.
- How: Use your own nail clippers, files, and other tools, and avoid sharing them with others.

Use Proper Nail Care Techniques

- Why: Improper techniques can cause damage and increase the risk of infection.
- How: Avoid cutting cuticles, biting nails, or using unclean tools.

Recognize Signs of Infection

- Symptoms: Redness, swelling, pain, and pus around the nail can indicate an infection.
- Action: If you notice signs of infection, seek medical advice promptly to prevent it from worsening.

Maintaining Overall Nail Health

Balanced Diet

- Why: Proper nutrition supports nail health and strength.
- How: Include foods rich in vitamins and minerals, such as biotin, zinc, and iron. Eat a balanced diet with plenty of fruits, vegetables, lean proteins, and whole grains.

Avoiding Harsh Chemicals

- Why: Chemicals can weaken and damage nails.

- How: Limit exposure to nail polish removers with acetone, and use nail-friendly products when possible.

Regular Manicures and Pedicures

- Why: Professional nail care can help maintain healthy nails and address any issues.
- How: Schedule regular appointments with a reputable nail technician who follows proper hygiene practices.

Personal Hygiene During Puberty

Understanding Bodily Changes

Puberty is a time of significant physical, hormonal, and emotional changes. These transformations often lead to new hygiene challenges, making it essential to adapt your personal care routines to accommodate these changes.

Physical Changes in Puberty

Hormonal Changes

- Why: Increased levels of hormones such as oestrogen and testosterone affect various bodily functions and can lead to new hygiene needs.
- Effects: Hormonal fluctuations can cause increased oil production, sweating, and changes in body odour.

Sweat and Body Odour

- Why: Puberty triggers the development of apocrine sweat glands, which produce a thicker sweat that bacteria break down into odour-causing compounds.
- Effects: You may notice a stronger body odour, especially in the armpits and groyne area.

Skin Changes

- Why: Increased oil production can lead to acne and other skin issues.
- Effects: The skin may become more oily, leading to clogged pores and acne.

Hair Growth

- Why: Puberty triggers the growth of body and facial hair due to increased hormone levels.
- Effects: Hair may begin to appear in areas such as the armpits, pubic region, and face.

Genital Changes

- Why: Growth and development in the genital area occur, leading to increased sensitivity and the need for specific hygiene practices.
- Effects: The genital area may produce more sweat and require careful cleaning to prevent infections.

Special Hygiene Tips for Boys and Girls

For Boys

Managing Body Odour

- Use Antiperspirant/Deodorant: Apply a good-quality antiperspirant or deodorant daily to manage sweat and body odour. Choose a product that suits your skin type and activity level.
- Daily Showering: Shower daily, especially after physical activities, to remove sweat and bacteria. Use an antibacterial soap to help reduce body odour.

Handling Acne

- Cleansing Routine: Use a gentle facial cleanser twice a day to keep your skin clean and prevent acne. Avoid scrubbing too hard, which can irritate the skin.

- Avoid Touching Your Face: Minimise touching your face to prevent transferring oils and bacteria from your hands to your skin.

Hair Care

- Regular Washing: Wash your hair regularly to manage excess oil and prevent dandruff. Choose a shampoo suited to your hair type.
- Facial Hair: If you begin to grow facial hair, decide whether to shave or trim it based on your preference. Use clean razors and shaving cream to avoid irritation.

Genital Hygiene

- Daily Cleaning: Wash the genital area daily with mild soap and water. Ensure you clean underneath the foreskin (if uncircumcised) and dry thoroughly.

- Wearing Breathable Underwear: Choose underwear made of breathable fabrics like cotton to reduce moisture and prevent irritation.

For Girls

Managing Body Odour

- Use Antiperspirant/Deodorant: Apply antiperspirant or deodorant to manage sweat and body odour. Opt for a product that works with your skin type and activity level.
- Daily Showering: Shower daily to remove sweat and bacteria. Use an antibacterial soap, especially in areas prone to sweating.

Handling Acne

- Cleansing Routine: Use a gentle, non-comedogenic facial cleanser to keep

your skin clean and prevent acne. Avoid over-cleansing or using harsh products.
- Avoid Touching Your Face: Refrain from touching your face frequently to reduce the risk of transferring oils and bacteria.

Hair Care

- Regular Washing: Wash your hair regularly to manage oil and keep it clean. Select a shampoo that suits your hair type and needs.
- Managing Menstrual Hair Growth: If you choose to manage hair growth in the bikini area, use a method that suits your comfort level, such as shaving, waxing, or trimming.

Menstrual Hygiene

- Using Sanitary Products: Use sanitary pads, tampons, or menstrual cups to manage menstrual flow. Choose products that suit your needs and comfort.

- Changing Products Regularly: Change sanitary products every few hours to maintain hygiene and prevent odours.
- Washing Hands: Always wash your hands before and after changing menstrual products to avoid infections.

Genital Hygiene

- Daily Cleaning: Clean the genital area daily with mild soap and water. Avoid douching, which can disrupt the natural balance of bacteria and yeast.
- Wearing Breathable Underwear: Opt for cotton underwear to keep the area dry and reduce moisture buildup.

General Hygiene Tips for Both Boys and Girls

Establish a Routine

- Why: A consistent hygiene routine helps manage body odour, skin health, and overall cleanliness.
- How: Set specific times for showering, brushing teeth, and other hygiene practices to build habits.

Hydration and Diet

- Why: Staying hydrated and eating a balanced diet supports skin health and overall well-being.
- How: Drink plenty of water and eat a diet rich in fruits, vegetables, and whole grains.

Managing Stress

- Why: Stress can affect skin health and increase sweating.
- How: Practise stress-management techniques like exercise, relaxation exercises, and adequate sleep.

Seeking Medical Advice

Why: Persistent skin problems, unusual odours, or discomfort may require medical attention. How: Consult a healthcare professional if you experience significant hygiene-related issues or concerns.

Clothing and Laundry Hygiene

Choosing Clean Clothes

Importance of Wearing Clean Clothes

- Health and Hygiene: Clean clothes help prevent the buildup of bacteria, fungi, and other microorganisms that can lead to skin infections and unpleasant odours.
- Comfort and Confidence: Wearing clean clothes contributes to overall comfort and enhances self-esteem, allowing you to feel fresh and confident throughout the day.
- Preventing Skin Issues: Clean clothing helps prevent skin conditions like rashes,

acne, and irritation that can result from wearing dirty or sweaty garments.

How to Choose Clean Clothes

Assessing Cleanliness

- Visual Inspection: Check clothes for visible dirt, stains, or spots. If a garment looks dirty, it's time for a wash.
- Smell Test: If clothes have an unpleasant odour, even if they appear clean, they should be washed. Odours can be a sign of bacteria or sweat buildup.
- Fit and Feel: Clothes that feel damp, sticky, or uncomfortable are likely in need of laundering, especially if they have been worn during physical activities.

Frequency of Washing

- Everyday Wear: Items like shirts, underwear, and socks should be washed

after each wear to maintain cleanliness and prevent odour.
- Outerwear and Jeans: Outerwear like jackets and jeans can be worn multiple times before washing, unless they become visibly soiled or start to smell.

Special Considerations

- Sportswear: Athletic clothing, including workout gear and uniforms, should be washed after each use due to sweat and bacteria.
- Undergarments: Always wear clean undergarments daily and change them after activities that cause excessive sweating or soiling.

Selecting the Right Clothing for Hygiene

Breathable Fabrics

- Why: Fabrics that allow air to circulate help keep your skin dry and reduce the risk of odour and irritation.
- How: Opt for natural fibres like cotton or moisture-wicking materials that help manage sweat and enhance comfort.

Proper Fit

- Why: Well-fitting clothes prevent chafing and irritation, which can occur with garments that are too tight or too loose.
- How: Choose clothing that fits comfortably without excessive tightness or looseness, especially in areas prone to sweat.

How to Properly Wash and Store Your Clothes

Washing Clothes

Sorting Laundry

- Why: Sorting helps prevent colour bleeding and ensures that each type of fabric is washed under the right conditions.
- How: Separate laundry into categories such as whites, colours, and delicates. Wash heavily soiled items separately from lightly soiled ones.

Choosing the Right Detergent

Types of Detergent:
- Liquid Detergent: Works well for pre-treating stains and is effective in all water temperatures.
- Powder Detergent: Ideal for white clothes and heavy-duty cleaning.
- High-Efficiency Detergent: Specifically formulated for high-efficiency washers, which use less water.
- Allergies and Sensitivities: If you have sensitive skin, opt for hypoallergenic or

fragrance-free detergents to avoid irritation.

Washing Techniques

- Temperature Settings: Use cold water for bright colours and delicate fabrics to prevent shrinking and colour bleeding. Warm water can be used for heavily soiled items and whites to help remove stains and odours.
- Cycle Settings: Choose the appropriate washing cycle based on the fabric type—delicate cycles for fragile items and regular cycles for durable fabrics.
- Pre-Treatment: Apply stain remover to stains before washing to enhance cleaning effectiveness. Gently rub the stain remover into the fabric and let it sit for a few minutes before laundering.

Drying Clothes

- Air Drying: Helps preserve the integrity of fabrics and is gentler on clothes. Hang clothes on a drying rack or clothesline to dry.
- Machine Drying: Use the dryer for items that require it, but be mindful of fabric care labels. Choose the appropriate heat setting to avoid shrinkage and damage.
- Avoid Over-Drying: Over-drying can weaken fabric fibres and cause shrinking. Remove clothes from the dryer while still slightly damp to minimise damage.

Storing Clothes

Proper Storage Practices

- Clean Clothes Before Storing: Always wash clothes before storing them to remove any residual dirt, sweat, or odours.
- Use Appropriate Hangers: Use padded or plastic hangers for delicate items and

wooden hangers for heavier garments to maintain their shape.
- Store in a Dry, Cool Place: Keep clothes in a dry, cool environment to prevent mould, mildew, and pests. Avoid storing clothes in damp or humid areas.

Seasonal Storage

- Off-Season Clothes: Store out-of-season clothing in breathable garment bags or containers to protect them from dust, insects, and moisture. Ensure they are clean and completely dry before storage.
- Rotate Wardrobe: Rotate your wardrobe seasonally to keep frequently worn clothes easily accessible and off-season items stored properly.

Maintaining Fabric Quality

- Avoid Direct Sunlight: Store clothes away from direct sunlight to prevent fading and degradation of fabric fibres.

- Use Moth Repellents: For natural fibres like wool, consider using moth repellents or cedar blocks to deter pests.

Regular Maintenance

- Check for Damage: Regularly inspect stored clothing for any signs of damage, pests, or mildew. Address issues promptly to avoid further damage.
- Freshen Up: Occasionally refresh stored clothes with fabric spray or by airing them out to maintain a pleasant smell and prevent mustiness.

Hygiene on the Go

Maintaining good hygiene while you're on the move—whether at school, during sports, or while travelling—can be challenging but is crucial for staying comfortable and healthy. This section provides practical tips and strategies for managing hygiene in various situations and outlines how to build an effective portable hygiene kit.

Hygiene Tips for School, Sports, and Travel

1. Hygiene Tips for School

Hand Hygiene

- Frequent Hand Washing: Wash your hands regularly with soap and water, especially before eating and after using the restroom. If soap and water aren't available, use hand sanitizer with at least 60% alcohol.
- Hand Hygiene Stations: Take advantage of hand sanitizer stations in common areas like classrooms and cafeterias. If your school doesn't have these, consider keeping a small bottle of hand sanitizer in your backpack.

Managing Body Odour

- Daily Showering: Ensure you shower daily to manage body odour and stay fresh throughout the school day.
- Deodorant: Apply deodorant or antiperspirant in the morning to control body odour. Consider using a travel-sized product for quick touch-ups if needed.
- Breathable Clothing: Wear clean, breathable fabrics like cotton to help

reduce sweat and odour. Change clothes if you notice any buildup of sweat or odour.

Keeping Your School Supplies Clean

- Clean Your Backpack: Regularly clean your backpack by wiping down its interior and exterior with disinfectant wipes. Avoid overloading it to ensure proper airflow and prevent mould.
- Sanitise Personal Items: Regularly clean personal items like pens, pencils, and notebooks with disinfectant wipes to minimise the spread of germs.

2. Hygiene Tips for Sports

Pre-Activity Hygiene

- Shower Before Sports: Shower before participating in sports to remove sweat and bacteria from your skin, which helps prevent skin infections and unpleasant odours.

- Wear Clean Gear: Ensure all sports gear, including uniforms and shoes, is clean before use. This helps reduce the risk of fungal infections and unpleasant smells.

During Activity

- Stay Hydrated: Drink water regularly to stay hydrated and help regulate body temperature. Proper hydration can also reduce sweat buildup.
- Manage Sweat: Use sweat-wicking clothing and headbands to keep sweat away from your face and body. Change into clean clothes after practice or games if possible.

Post-Activity Hygiene

- Shower After Sports: Shower as soon as possible after physical activities to remove sweat, dirt, and bacteria from your skin. Use antibacterial soap to help prevent skin infections.

- Clean Equipment: Wipe down and disinfect sports equipment and gear after use to minimise the spread of germs. Air out equipment and allow it to dry completely.

3. Hygiene Tips for Travel

Maintaining Cleanliness While Travelling

- Hand Hygiene: Use hand sanitizer frequently, especially before eating and after touching public surfaces. Carry travel-sized hand sanitizer and disinfectant wipes in your bag.
- Avoid Touching Your Face: Minimise touching your face, particularly your eyes, nose, and mouth, to reduce the risk of transferring germs.

Managing Personal Space

- Clean Surfaces: Use disinfectant wipes to clean surfaces in public transportation,

such as aeroplane trays, bus seats, and train handles.
- Use Personal Items: Bring your own travel pillow, blanket, and utensils to avoid direct contact with potentially unclean surfaces.

Staying Fresh

- Travel Hygiene Kit: Pack a small hygiene kit with essentials like deodorant, facial wipes, dry shampoo, and a toothbrush and toothpaste for quick freshening up.
- Change of Clothes: Keep a change of clothes in your carry-on bag to change into if needed. Opt for breathable fabrics to stay comfortable during long journeys.

Building a Portable Hygiene Kit

A portable hygiene kit ensures you have the essentials you need to maintain cleanliness and freshness while on the go. Here's how to assemble an effective hygiene kit:

1. Essential Items for the Kit

Hand Sanitizer

- Purpose: For hand cleaning when soap and water are not available.
- Tip: Choose a small, travel-sized bottle that meets TSA regulations if travelling by air.

Disinfectant Wipes

- Purpose: For wiping down surfaces and cleaning hands when soap is not accessible.
- Tip: Opt for wipes that are gentle on skin and effective against germs.

Deodorant

- Purpose: To manage body odour throughout the day.

- Tip: Use a travel-sized roll-on or stick deodorant for easy portability.

Facial Wipes

- Purpose: For quick facial cleanups to remove sweat, oil, and dirt.
- Tip: Choose wipes that are suitable for your skin type, especially if you have sensitive skin.

Dry Shampoo

- Purpose: To freshen up hair and absorb excess oil without needing to wash it.
- Tip: Select a small, travel-sized canister for easy use.

Toothbrush and Toothpaste

- Purpose: For maintaining oral hygiene while on the go.
- Tip: Use a compact, travel-size toothbrush and a small tube of toothpaste.

Hand Cream

- Purpose: To keep hands moisturised, especially if using hand sanitizer frequently.
- Tip: Choose a small, non-greasy hand cream that fits easily in your bag.

Small Towel or Washcloth

- Purpose: For personal use to freshen up or clean up spills.
- Tip: Opt for a lightweight, quick-drying towel.

2. Packing Your Kit

- Choose a Compact Bag: Use a small, clear zippered bag or a compact toiletry bag to keep all items organised and easily accessible.
- Label Items: If travelling internationally, consider labelling items in different

languages or include any necessary customs documentation for liquids.
- Keep It Updated: Regularly check and refill your hygiene kit to ensure all items are in good condition and replace any used or expired products.

3. Customising Your Kit

- Personal Needs: Tailor your hygiene kit based on your personal preferences and specific needs. For example, if you have specific skincare or allergy requirements, include appropriate products.
- Activity-Specific Items: If you engage in specific activities like hiking or swimming, include additional items such as insect repellent or swimwear hygiene products.

Printed in Great Britain
by Amazon